Different Like ME

Written by **Xochitl Dixon**   Illustrated by **Bonnie Lui**

Our Daily Bread
Publishing™

Different Like Me

© 2020 by Xochitl E. Dixon

All rights reserved.

Author is represented by the literary agency of Credo Communications, LLC, Grand Rapids, Michigan, www.credocommunications.net.

Requests for permission to quote from this book should be directed to: Permissions Department, Our Daily Bread Publishing, PO Box 3566, Grand Rapids, MI 49501, or contact us by email at permissionsdept@odb.org.

Scripture quotations are from the Holy Bible, New International Version®, NIV® Copyright © 1973, 1978, 1984, 2011 by Biblica, Inc.™ Used by permission of Zondervan. All rights reserved worldwide. www.zondervan.com.

Interior design by Kris Nelson/StoryLook Design

Library of Congress Cataloging-in-Publication Data

Names: Dixon, Xochitl, author. | Lui, Bonnie, illustrator.
Title: Different like me / written by Xochitl Dixon ; illustrated by Bonnie
    Lui.
Description: Grand Rapids, Michigan : Our Daily Bread Publishing, 2020. |
    Audience: Grades K-1 | Summary: "Celebrate differences and uncover what
    we have in common on this whimsical journey of discovering we're all
    part of God's wonderful creation"-- Provided by publisher.
Identifiers: LCCN 2020010092 | ISBN 9781640700420 (hardcover)
Subjects: LCSH: Creation--Juvenile literature. | Cultural
    pluralism--Religious aspects--Christianity--Juvenile literature. |
    Social acceptance--Religious aspects--Christianity--Juvenile literature.
Classification: LCC BS651 .D59 2020 | DDC 231.7/65--dc23
LC record available at https://lccn.loc.gov/2020010092

Printed in the United States of America

21 22 23 24 25 26 27 / 8 7 6 5 4 3 2

"So God created mankind in his own image,
in the image of God he created them;
male and female he created them."

GENESIS 1:27

I look all around me
and what do I see?
So many kids who are
different from me.

Different shades. Different hair. Different eyes. Different smiles.

Even our bodies
are all different styles.

We speak different languages.
Some talk with their hands.
Some come from next door
Some from faraway lands.

I look all around me
and what do I see?
So many kids who are
different from me.

We have different families,
Different friends, homes, and names.
   We like different pets, different foods, different games.

Some kids like to throw.
Some kids like to catch.

Some want to stand out.

And some want to match.

Some act out adventures
of dragons and kings.

Some like to paint pictures
of all sorts of things.

I look all around me
and what do I see?

So many kids who are different from me.

Some use a wheelchair.
Some see with a cane.

But while we are different . . . we *feel* things the same.

We feel happy and hurried.

We feel scared.
We feel sad.

We feel grumpy and worried.

We feel free.
We feel glad.

I look all around me and what do I see?
So many kids, not so different from me.

We all laugh and act silly.
We hurt and we cry.

We bounce with excitement.
We hide and act shy.

We're all good at something,
and have kindness to share.

We can all be good helpers,
who love and who care.

I look all around me and what do I see?
God made every kid different . . .

and special, like me!

"For you created my inmost being;
you knit me together in my mother's womb.
I praise you because I am fearfully and wonderfully made;
your works are wonderful, I know that full well."

PSALM 139:13–14

Dear Parent or Teacher:

In a world where many people mock the differences of others, *Different Like Me* assures children that God intentionally created each person to be unique and to work together. By learning to rejoice in our Maker's wonderful creativity, we can discover our purposes as God's masterpieces, both individually and in community. This confidence can nurture a healthy and holy appreciation and understanding of our differences as well as the sameness that connects us.

Children are not exempt from the wounds of verbal and physical attacks based on their differences. Abolishing negative stereotypes can empower children to stand against bullying that has too often escalated to criminal offenses and self-harm. Embracing the beauty of diversity at a young age can equip children to celebrate the uniqueness of others and affirm the specialness of all the people God created and loves.

These questions can help you have important conversations with your children:

1. (Read Genesis 1) What does the Bible say about all the things God created?

2. (Read Ephesians 2:10) Why do you think God created everyone different?

3. Have you ever thought being different was bad? Why or why not?

4. When have you disliked being different from someone else? When have you enjoyed being unique?

5. How would you feel if someone teased you for being different? How do you think others feel when they're teased for being different?

6. How did God make you different from your best friend or friends? How did God make you the same as your best friend or friends?

7. How can God use your differences to help you work better together?

8. How can you celebrate your friends and the ways they are different like you?

9. Who else do you think would like to read *Different Like Me*?

I dedicate *Different Like Me* to my beautifully diverse family, especially my unique and amazing husband, Alan, and sons, A.J. and Xavier, to my wonderfully-made and God-chosen friends who remind me that being different is cool, and to every person who has ever felt weird, out of place, or misunderstood. I'm so glad God created each and every one of you to be different . . . like me!

Special thanks to Bonnie Lui for sharing her heart through the gorgeous illustrations in *Different Like Me,* to Patsy Ann Taylor, the first person who encouraged me to share *Different Like Me* with readers, to my mom, Martha Gutierrez, who taught me how to appreciate picture books and love all people through my words and actions, and to the *Tails for Life* family, especially Jacob and Amanda Guell, who help Callie and me learn to serve the Lord together.

—Xochitl E. Dixon